Beauty of
New Jersey

A wee reminder of your
New Jersey visit. Come back
again soon.

Fondly,

Edith and Catherine

Beauty of
New Jersey

Text: Paul M. Lewis
Concept & Design: Robert D. Shangle

Revised Edition
First Printing October, 1991
Published by LTA Publishing Company
2735 S.E. Raymond Street, Portland, Oregon 97202
Robert D. Shangle, Publisher

"Learn about America in a beautiful way."

This book features the photography of
James Blank
Shangle Photographics

Library of Congress Cataloging-in-Publication Data

Lewis, Paul M.
    Beauty of New Jersey / text, Paul M. Lewis; concept & design, Robert D. Shangle.
        p.   cm.
    Revised edition of: Beautiful New Jersey / concept and design, Robert D. Shangle;
text, Paul M. Lewis. c1980.
    ISBN 0-917630-85-8 (hardbound): $19.95. — ISBN 0-917630-84-X (paperback):
$9.95
    1. New Jersey — Description and travel — 1981 — Views. I. Shangle, Robert D.
II. Beautiful New Jersey. III. Title.
F135.B38   1991
917.4904'43 — dc20   91-25684
                                                                            CIP

Production, Concept and Distribution by LTA Publishing Company, Portland, Oregon.
Printed in Thailand. This book produced as the major component of the "World Peace and
Understanding" program of Beauty of America Printing Company, Portland, Oregon.

Contents

Introduction

People have been saying mean things about New Jersey for a long time — ever since they discovered it made a handy connector between the great population centers of the East Coast. The migratory hordes who zoom through on the freeways or the trains en route to New York and New England, or to Philadelphia and cities farther south, tend to think of the state as all rails and roadways. So New Jersey gets a bad press from being a good pathway. The notion that it may very well be something else besides seems to be regarded by otherwise reasonable people as the imaginative puffery of the state's tourist promoters.

Even more than the riders on Amtrak's fast and busy tracks through New Jersey's middle, armies of motorists take to those turnpikes like flies to flypaper. A lot of them seem to be stuck there, because they never get off and look around. Those that do suddenly see, because they have begun to look, that there's a New Jersey looking back at them with a different face from the one they thought was all she had.

The contrasts for which Jersey is not-so-famous begin to reveal themselves as soon as the pace slows down and the expressway exit ramps take you out in the "back country." This variety begins with some basic, and rather remarkable, statistics relative to size and land use. New Jersey is at the smaller end of the scale in land area, 46th among the states. Its 8,204 square miles are home to about 7,800,000 persons. People go where jobs are, and New Jersey offers its citizens a great number and diversity of livelihoods. The state has well over 14,000 manufacturing plants and is a leading producer of chemicals, clothing, metals, machinery, electronics, rubber plastics, stone, textiles, processed food, farm crops, paper, books, and a few hundred other things.

New Jersey's fertile farms have long been appreciated by Philadelphians, although not many stop to look at them on their way to the summer beach resorts. The loamy soil of the southwest around Camden has been the purveyor for years beyond memory of big, beautiful Jersey tomatoes, tender golden corn, succulent melons, and many other delectables to the plates of Pennsylvanians (and others) across the Delaware River. This brings up another statistic: more than 24 percent of New Jersey — some 1,025,000 acres — is devoted to farms. Another 40 percent is forested. The latter figure may surprise those whose only news of New Jersey is of something momentous in Newark, Elizabeth, East Orange, or Jersey City, or what's happening at the Atlantic City casinos. The big towns overwhelm the smaller towns by sheer numbers, making news by just being there. But that is why the Minnesotan, Indianan, Nebraskan, or Nevadan may look sceptical when told that New Jersey has wilderness, mountains, big forest preserves watered by the purest streams, ski slopes, historic old towns, hundreds of lakes and ponds, pristine swamplands set aside as game refuges, and the longest extent of magnificent white-sand beach in the world on its 127-mile coastline. Speaking of the shore, Atlantic City may seem to be the whole show to outsiders; but of course this isn't so. Atlantic City's fame makes it a perennial contender for the Miss World of resort communities, so it gets a disproportionate share of the limelight.

Because New Jersey is so up-to-date, we may tend to forget that she's old fashioned, too. Old towns are spotted around the northern hills and the southern coastal plains, reminders of the state's historical importance. It was, after all, one of the 13 original states, after having been the most fought-over battleground of the War of Independence. The motto, "Crossroads of the Revolution," is New Jersey's by right. Nearly a hundred engagements took place within its borders. Historic parks, where Washington's armies were encamped, and buildings, which have stood since those times of struggle and hardship, are among the hallowed symbols that make the state both a monument to the past and a model for the future.

New Jersey's vitality surely is one of the benefits of the variety of living space she offers — all the more remarkable because of her small portion of the world's land area. She is only 166 miles from High Point at the northern end to the tip of Cape May, and her average width is 55 miles. New Jersey cinches up her waist from Trenton across to Raritan Bay, measuring a mere 32 miles. But it's not really necessary to dwell on physical size, because it has never been all that important in the affairs of the world. Some of the tiniest parts of it have cast the longest shadow, which may be a good way to sum up this big-little state. Human history has turned on events in New Jersey, and through the years, the state's importance has grown to the point where what happens here reaches around the world. Her vast industrial might has produced one of the best standards of living in the country, yet her natural inheritance is still in good order, much the same as it was when the country was new.

P.M.L.

Where Everything's Happening

Northeast New Jersey is a very busy place. Most of the state's population is established in this long, narrow corridor that spreads south past Raritan Bay and halfway to Trenton in the "belt." Cities and towns are so thick that all the open space has been gobbled up. The big industrial cities are Newark, Jersey City, Paterson, Elizabeth, and Bayonne, amid a sea of smaller working towns. Bedroom communities for New York City lie west of the George Washington Bridge, Lincoln Tunnel, and Holland Tunnel. Their proximity to Wonderful Town across the Hudson gives them people power without much of an industrial base. There is Hackensack, with all its Bergen County sisters and brothers: Teaneck, Bergenfield, Englewood, Fort Lee, and so on. Together with the industrial cities, they add up to two-thirds of the state's 7,800,000 citizens. Quite a few souls to jam into a few square miles.

Although economic drives are what make these towns go, they are not the whole story. Places like Paterson, Elizabeth, and Newark have grown old with the state and their history is a living presence. The Passaic River wanders through this corner, making a great loop around some of its towns before it empties into Newark Bay. Paterson is one of the places the river passes through on this serpentine journey, performing a spectacular leap at this point. The Great Falls of the Passaic rumble ponderously over a wide, curving ledge in the old mill district of the city, with an authority rivaling Niagara. These days the falls are a splendid scenic backdrop to industrial Paterson. Once upon a time, they were more than that, providing power for the looms of Paterson's silk factories that attracted great waves of Arabic immigrant workers. In 1961 the falls became a national historic site, the centerpiece of the Passaic S.U.M. Historic District embracing many of the old factories and streets around the river. Some of the dusky-red brick plants and other buildings have been restored and some are still in the process. Alexander Hamilton started things off in the right direction in 1791 with his suggestion for the S.U.M. (Society for Establishing Useful Manufactures) — the beginnings of Paterson as an industrial city, which was one of the first steps of the infant nation toward manufacturing independence. Hamilton and his New Jersey colleagues saw the immense potential of the powerful Passaic River, and Paterson was on its way. Today Hamilton's statue gazes down at the falls from a high perch on the river bank. The old and the new crowd the scene, symbolizing the city's potent industrial clout and her historic role in the evolution.

Elizabeth was once a ward of Essex County, but when the town began to grow big like Newark, the county's chief city, Elizabethans decided in 1857 to form their own kingdom, calling it Union County. Essex County's rival was slow to develop, but early in this century, industries began a mass invasion. Oil refineries were established at Linden-Rahway, growing over the year into one of the largest such complexes in the world. Diversity is the key to the success of Elizabeth and other Union County communities. Chemicals, drugs, research laboratories, auto assembly plants, and other assorted industries have spread their houses over the hills and plains to the west, in towns whose names are descriptive of the land itself, like Westfield, Springfield, Hillside, Plainfield, and Scotch Plain (the last two settled by Scots who came west from Perth Amboy in the 1680s).

The heavy industrialization of Union County's towns and the fast flow of people into the area since the 1900s have meant not only the filling in of open spaces, but the rapid disappearance of much that was preliminary to that phenomenal growth. History has been treated rather roughly — many of Union's early monuments are no more. But here and there something survives. Elizabeth does the right thing by remembering its place as New Jersey's first English-speaking settlement. As Elizabethtown it was also the state's first capital. So, even while today it is the capital of just Union County, it shows its class by making sure some of its links with the early days are kept around. Founded in 1664, it has been the home of some famous people, from Alexander Hamilton, Revolutionary War hero and first Secretary of the Treasury, to Admiral William "Bull" Halsey, of World War II. Many of the homes and buildings of the Revolutionary period and later are preserved in Elizabeth, so that historical perspective is an important part of its modern life.

Hudson is the smallest county in the area and one of the biggest in population and economic pizzazz. The county's long north-south axis stretches about 14 miles along the Hudson River. The area is urban, with big towns like Jersey City, Hoboken, Union City, and Bayonne. Transportation was what finally made Hudson County get serious, after years of being a playland for wealthy New Yorkers. The railroads brought with them concentrations of heavy industry, attracting immigrant labor and building up the population. The swarms of ethnic workers who came to run the 19th-century railroads and factories put their stamp on the town they had made big. Jersey City was the railroad hub, where the Irish congregated. Germans were attracted to Hoboken and the cities of north Hudson. The mills of Harrison and Kearny brought the Scottish. During the 20th century, the population blend of many northeast Jersey towns has been altered by the tidal waves of Italians, who arrived seeking opportunity. Bayonne, down in the "neck," was once a favorite sanctuary of New York society, who had turned its bay frontage into a retreat of the wealthy. In the last quarter of the 19th century, the big oil companies moved in with their oil refineries and that was the end of Bayonne-by-the-Bay.

Newark is the state's biggest city, and one of the oldest, as well. It was already a village of substance when Essex County was formed in 1682. Some time before this, the town had adopted its present name, Newark, or "New Work." While Newark was growing during the early 18th century by the Passaic River, some of its settlers moved into the meadows and hills of western Essex County and set up farming communities, which became the present-day towns there — West Orange, East Orange. Montclair, and Bloomfield. In 1748 Newark became the founding site of the College of New Jersey, which eventually acquired a new name and a prestigious reputation after its move to Princeton in 1756. The Morris Canal, which still exists more-or-less complete across northern New Jersey, was finished in 1832, helping Newark onto the industrial track. Maritime transport into Newark Bay, and railroad building, gave "genteel" Newark another push toward industrialization and big-city status.

After the Civil War Newark's population went over the 100,000 figure and it was on its way. The diverse ethnic labor force, so important to northeast New Jersey's economic development, came into the city, attracted by its clothing and leather manufactures, iron works, locomotives, carriages, shoes, jewelry — a great smorgasbord of enterprises that brought in the Irish, Germans, Poles, and Italians to join the "old-timers." While Newark was bursting its seams, outlying Essex Country communities were attracting home buyers because of easy access by train, trolley, and after the turn of the century, by car. One of those homes, in

West Orange, belonged to inventor Thomas A. Edison. He not only lived in West Orange for a time (his home is still there), but he opened a research laboratory in 1887 and a phonographic firm in 1890.

The marvelous transportation system, which ties the city and county to the rest of the world, is all the more valuable economically because of Newark's fine location within the biggest single population ring in the nation. The growing importance of big and modern Newark Airport for the East Coast is one aspect of this. The airport is being used more and more for travel to and from New York because it is handier for many travelers than that city's La Guardia and John F. Kennedy airports.

Essex is among the most populous of counties, and its open land is by now mainly a memory. But some, miraculously, has been preserved. The western part has big South Mountain and Eagle Rock reservations, and across the Passaic from Newark is Branch Brook Park, looking like a transplant from the lake country of Morris County to the west.

Bergen county is the most "bedroomy" part of the crowded northeast. The George Washington Bridge, completed over the Hudson River in 1931, turned the county into a commuter's heaven, changing its farmland into home sites. The New York Dutch were probably the first commuters, establishing a trading post in 1618 across the river from their settlement of New Amsterdam. The Dutch were latecomers, however, being preceded in Bergen by the Hackensack Indians. The Hackensacks made things easy for those early white settlers, thereby launching cross-river relationships with Manhattan, which have grown quite close.

Bergen County has no really big towns, being like one big town itself. The county covers 233 square miles, and occupying most of that space are 70 separate communities. New Milford was the first on the scene in 1677. Its founder was a French Huguenot, who thus upstaged both the

Dutch and the English. But Hackensack, farther downstream on the big Hackensack River, grew up faster and became the county seat. It was both a port for ocean-going ships and the center of a thriving farm region. The whole county was an agricultural wonder during the 19th century, producing foodstuffs of extraordinary size and quality from its river-bottom soil. Because Bergen has become an area of homes more than factories, it has more of the amenities. Parks, lakes, and reservations give it an exceptional level of livability. The most familiar of Bergen's natural features are the Palisades, in Palisades Interstate Park, those steep, ragged cliffs along the Hudson that give the New York side of the Hudson such an eyeful. Lower Bergen also has the Meadowlands, once less elegantly referred to as the Jersey Swamps by travelers passing in their vicinity. The pig farms along the river had an overpowering "presence," which always extended strong greetings unless one could suspend breathing until past the area. That is all gone now. Where the pigs and garbage once inhabited the 500 or so acres along the Hackensack is now a fancy and much better smelling development of high-rise apartments, stores, businesses, and all that pertains thereto. And Meadowlands is now the name of a giant sports complex near East Rutherford. There's a racetrack, a football stadium, and a basketball arena, all in heroic scale befitting heroic accomplishments by equine and human athletes, on the field and the floor.

Fort Lee, by the Washington Bridge, has had a varied career. The river-bank town was "Hollywood" for a time, before the film industry moved to the West Coast. Big names made famous motion pictures here in the first quarter of this century. The steep escarpment of the Palisades was a marvelous setting for the once-popular movie serials like "The Perils of Pauline," with Pearl White. But Fort Lee has been more than make-believe. It has its memories of the Revolutionary era, now enshrined in Fort Lee Historic Park with its reconstructed gun batteries and museum. In River Edge, near Hackensack, stands another reminder of other times: the Von Steuben House. A pre-Revolutionary structure, the dwelling was given to Baron Von Steuben by the United States for his exceptional help in building the Patriot army. Now publicly owned, it contains not only relics of the Colonial days, but Indian artifacts as well.

Two counties share New Jersey's narrow "waistline." Although this area is part of the transportation belt, it is not all that citified. Raritan Bay is at one end and the Delaware River at the other. Perth Amboy is at the Raritan end and Trenton, the state capital, on the Delaware side. Middlesex and Mercer, the counties in question, manage to be relatively uncrowded, although there is another big town here, too. New Brunswick is on the Raritan River. Like Perth Amboy, it antedates the Revolution. Perth Amboy was, for a long time, the provincial East Jersey capital, where the royal governors lived. But after Independence, New Brunswick became the Middlesex County center. A little institution of learning had been established there in 1771, by the Dutch Reformed Church. Named Queens College, it had one faculty member in the beginning, and one graduate in its first class. The college moved about a lot during the war and went into suspended animation off and on until 1825. Then Henry Rutgers, a New Yorker, put it on a more-or-less solid footing back in New Brunswick with some solid cash. Rutgers, now the New Jersey state university, is still there, and has become one of the nation's most esteemed centers of learning, with a Nobel laureate among its latter-day distinctions.

Before Thomas A. Edison decamped in 1887 for West Orange up north, he made things happen in a little rural village in upper Middlesex. The "Wizard of Menlo Park" set up the country's first research lab in 1876.

Atlantic City

Ironmasters Mansion, Batsto

Old Red Mill at Clinton

Atlantic City

The Wading River

Barnegat Lighthouse

In Allaire Village State Park

Historic Van Sykles Corner at Clinton

Wilk Farm, Morristown Battlefield National Historic Park

Ocean City

Historic Grange Building, Cold Spring

Musconetcong River near Waterloo Village

Marina at Trump Castle, Atlantic City

Cape May

Cape May

In The New Jersey Pine Barrens

Hereford Inlet Lighthouse

The Ford Mansion, Morristown Battlefield National Historic Site (George Washington's Headquarters)

On The Boardwalk, Atlantic City

Asbury Park

Sandy Hook Lighthouse

The New Jersey Pine Barrens

North of Stone Harbor

Atlantic City

Atlantic City

Soldiers' Huts, Morristown Battlefield National Historic Site

The Salem Oak, Over 500 Years Old, Salem

Sailing Off Highland

Near Salem

Barnegat Lighthouse Area

Gateway National Recreation Area

At Cold Spring on Cape May

At Batsto Village State Park

Liberty State Park, Jersey City

Atlantic City

Batsto Lake

Victorian Architecture, Cape May

Gateway National Recreation Area

Highland

Historic Waterloo Village

LIGHTHOUSE PARK
ATLANTIC ELECTRIC
BALLY'S PARK PLACE
BAYLY MARTIN & FAY
ROBERT J. CATALANO & ASSOCIATES
FALASCA PLG. HTG & CLG., INC.
FIRST JERSEY NATIONAL BANK SOUTH
GOLDEN NUGGET HOTEL CASINO
HARRAHS MARINA HOTEL CASINO
LABOV MECHANICAL CONTRACTORS
R.C. MAXWELL COMPANY
WILLIAM RAFFERTY FAMILY
SAFE & SOUND SECURITY CORP INC.
SCARPA ELECTRIC COMPANY
Radisson

Absecon Lighthouse, Atlantic City

Allaire Village State Park

Spruce Run State Park

In the New Jersey Pine Barrens

St. Peter by the Sea Church, Cape May

Lewes Ferry, Cape May

Lumpond State Park

In Menlo Park he came up with the phonograph, the incandescent bulb, and a passel of other inventions.

A great deal happens in Mercer County, next door on the west, largely because of Trenton, the state capital. But some of the most important happenings occurred before Mercer was carved out of the surrounding counties in 1838. The area's early growth was helped along considerably when the infant College of New Jersey was moved out of Newark to Princeton in 1756. With the arrival of the college, the neighborhood began to take on both cultural and warlike overtones. The campus quickly became a rallying ground for Colonial grievances against England. During the actual fighting, the region was an important battleground. Washington's celebrated crossing of the Delaware, on Christmas night in 1776, was the prelude to his equally celebrated victory at Trenton, shortly thereafter. Princeton was another victory for the continental Army, before the army moved to a winter encampment at Morristown. During the Princeton battle, Nassau Hall, the college's first building (1756), changed hands several times.

During the early years of the new century, Princeton College again became a battleground, this time between students and faculty. Nassau Hall still stands, although it was set ablaze in 1802 during one of these intramural wars. Princeton University has settled down since then and developed into one of the world's highly regarded institutions of learning. Some of the most noted scholars and creative thinkers have come to Princeton, including Albert Einstein, and, of course, Woodrow Wilson, president of the university before he became governor of New Jersey in 1911 and President of the United States in 1913. The town of Princeton is a suitable setting for its illustrious university. Its tree-lined streets and carefully tended estates give it a soft beauty that, some would say, makes Princeton the most handsome of college towns. One of those old and honored residences is Morven, built before the Revolution by Richard Stockton, a signer of the Declaration of Independence. It is now the official residence of the state's governor.

Trenton's welfare really depends very little on its role as the state capital. As most easterners know, Trenton is also an industrial powerhouse. Its diversified manufactures have made a truism of its motto, "Trenton Makes — The World Takes." But besides government and business, Trenton is history, and is pleased to let people see that side of itself. In old Trenton, for instance, there is the handsome 1719 home of William Trent, a town founder. The Old Barracks, vintage 1758, housed those Hessians who were surprised by Washington's troops on that morning of the First Battle of Trenton. The Barracks are located near the State House, a large domed structure that still has some traces within it of the original State House of 1792. For a while, back in those formative years, Trenton seemed on the way to becoming the capital of the whole country, but the choice of a north-south compromise city on the Potomac scuttled her romance.

West State Street, across the Capital complex, sums it all up nicely. A block of well-preserved 19th-century homes along the street offers a small-scale contrast to the grandeur of the governmental complex. Victorian, Federal, and Greek Revival architectural styles project a feeling of stability and dignity, which seems reassuring in our generally frantic times. The handsome homes are protected in the State House Historic District. Trenton's attention to its continuity with the past has helped it maintain a livability that is not always found in towns of such industrial prowess.

Camden is the other big Jersey town on the Delaware side. Although it has always had an image as that place across the river from

Philadelphia, the city is an industrial power in its own right and a marketplace for the produce of south Jersey. Shipping and shipbuilding crowd its docks, facing the Quaker City across the wide lower Delaware. Camden is also into soup, so to speak. The giant Campbells' Soup Company is a Camden enterprise, launched in 1869 when Joseph Campbell and partners began the packing of peas and tomatoes. Many residents commute to the Philadelphia area to work, contributing to Camden County's economy by spending their money there. Good-looking suburbs, such as Cherry Hill and Haddonfield, are favorite locations for many of the commuters.

Camden's busy industrial life long ago ended the ferry-town personality of the city. It has obliterated much of old-town Camden. But here and there are reminders that Camden is not just hustle and bustle. The town's most illustrious resident is still very much remembered. Walt Whitman, one of the greatest American poets, came to Camden to live in 1873. Until he died in 1892, he wrote and thrived amid the commotion of the fast-growing town. The house that he lived in during his final years is lovingly maintained. Nearby in Haddonfield is the Indian King Tavern, which goes much farther back. Built in 1750, after the Revolution, it became a favorite rendezvous of ferry-riding Philadelphians intent on discovering New Jersey. One of its soon-to-be-famous visitors was a beautiful and lively Quaker girl named Dorothea (Dolly) Payne, who achieved renown years later as the wife of President James Madison.

The Northwest Hills

In these days of fast everything, distances are more often measured in minutes than in miles. The scenic hill-and-lake country of north New Jersey is, quite literally, only minutes away from the industrial concentrations of the northeast. Yet relatively few people around the country are aware that this, too, is New Jersey, though some of them may live nearby. The way to cure such a regrettable state of mind, of course, is to take a few excursions around this rural corner. In early summer the heavily forested slopes stretch in all directions, clad in various shades of green. Even though you might be moving along Interstate Highway 80, the cross-state freeway, you almost get the impression of being on a country lane, so relaxing is that circular view of mountains and forests and lakes. In the fall it is even more spectacular, when the north Jersey hills burst forth in shamelessly gaudy reds, rusts, golds, and yellows at the first touch of frost. Then the cars crowd the roads, full of New Jerseyites who know a good thing when they see it.

Morris County is the centerpiece of all this, in both a historical and geographical sense. Morristown, the county seat, is an historical site all by itself. Morristowners need only step outside their doors to be onstage in a theater of history. The Ford Mansion, Washington's headquarters in Morristown, is part of a National Historical Park that includes Jockey

Hollow, the 1779-80 encampment area of the Continental Army five miles south of town. Use of the Ford Mansion was offered to General Washington by Mrs. Jacob Ford, Jr., when he moved his rag-tag army into winter quarters at Morristown, following brilliant victories at Trenton and Princeton. Mrs. Ford was the widow and daughter-in-law of two Morris County Patriot leaders and ironmasters, Jacob Sr. and Jr., both of whom had died in January, 1777. The Ford Mansion, built in 1774, was one of the most splendid homes in town. The house has been faithfully restored to its look and condition at the time of George and Martha's occupancy, even to some of the Fords' original furniture and the beds used by the various occupants. The bed length often times brings up the question: why were the camp beds and cots used by Washington's aides so short? The reason is that in those times, and especially during the harsh winter of 1780, people routinely slept in a semi-reclined position to alleviate bronchial distress. Pneumonia and tuberculosis took heavy tolls in those days.

Jockey Hollow, the large encampment area, was like Valley Forge in 1777-78, a terrible ordeal for the soldiers. The 10,000 men of the Continental Army lived in simple huts and endured constant cold, hunger, and sickness during that harsh winter. Walking through the meadows and young forests of this area now, the visitor who can imagine that time of harsh trial has reason to be astounded and moved by the courage, devotion, and sacrifice of those first American soldiers.

Morris County's hills and valleys are not quite as rural as they were during those beginning years, but there is still much open country. Forests have grown up again where earlier ones were turned into building timbers and firewood. A drive along the county's back roads is a tour though some of the East's most idyllic landscape. Hardwood stands, knolls and ridges, rolling vales, lakes, creeks, and rivers are there for the seeing, especially west and north of Morristown and Dover. Small communities are still the scale here, towns like Boonton and Mountain Lakes and Denville, close to the freeway, but hidden away from it by forests and hills. The towns are far away in personality, too, retreats from the sometimes-frantic business of making a living.

The wildlife likes Morris County towns, too. Deer and small game are often seen in the area. And the birds are almost as thick as the leaves on the trees. One of the most delightful times of day is early morning, when birds like to do their vocalizing. The varied bell tones of the warblers come pouring down from the tree tops in a refreshing splash of sound. The warblers are more often heard than seen, but many others of northern New Jersey's avian residents put in frequent appearances. Cardinals are among them, posing in their brilliant red plumage on the grass or on a flowering shrub. The scarlet tanagers seem more inclined to high acrobatics among the tree branches, with competition from the goldfinches, New Jersey's state bird.

The quiet is broken only by nature's noise, except for the big jet birds that pass over once in a while to and from their nest at Newark Airport. Even so, the feeling of another time is strong. There is a physical reminder of it nearby at the bottom of this Boonton hill. The Morris Canal passes through on its way across northern New Jersey. Parts of it have been filled in since the days when it was an important barge route. The canal is, at least to some extent, a child of the iron hills of Morris County. In the 18th and 19th centuries, the county was alight with the fires of iron forges by the Rockaway River. The forges got their ore from a few mines where outcropping "blackstone" made for easy digging. The biggest problems were the high cost of transportation and the fast depletion of forest around the forges. The Morris Canal solved these problems and brought

70

prosperity to iron-making towns like Dover, Boonton, and Rockaway. The canal's heyday didn't last long, however. Soon the mills were forging axles, wheels, and rails for the trains that would make the canal obsolete. There's talk about restoring the canal to some of its former glory. Whether that happens or not, the Morris Canal is a picturesque reminder of the time when the nation was just setting out on its career as an industrial power.

Mountain-ringed Lake Hopatcong, in western Morris County, is New Jersey's largest, its long shoreline stretching along the northern mountain divide. The lake is credited with having inspired George P. Macculoch with his plan for the Morris Canal, using waters of the lake to flow down the river valleys to the east and west. The lake is now the centerpiece of a state park and a recreational mecca for residents of the area. All of the usual water-related activities are available along its forest-edged length, in addition to the not-so-unusual one of ice-fishing in the wintertime. One of the towns along the lake shores is Stanhope, the address of Waterloo Village (named in honor of Wellington's defeat of Napoleon at Waterloo, Belgium, in 1815) became a busy inland port. A forge was built there, a grist and saw mill, a tavern, a store, and 15 dwellings. Since World War II, Waterloo Village has been undergoing a restoration and is open to the public now as a National Historic Site. Strolling through this quiet and handsome old place is a restorative in itself. The village street winds along the canal and the Musconetcong River, passing one fascinating structure after another. There's the General Store, the Grist Mill, the Blacksmith Shop, the Apothecary, various residences, and so on. Appropriately costumed employees of the Village Foundation welcome visitors, demonstrating some of the early Village occupations. The Grist Mill, for example, still grinds wheat into flour with its huge mill stones, using a system of sluices to turn a giant water wheel that powers the stones. Waterloo is one of the most remarkable of the many historic villages found on the East Coast.

Northwest New Jersey gets more mountainous the farther into it you get. Although the ridges are not very high, they dominate the landscape with their thickly forested shoulders. At the very northern tip of the state, in Sussex County, is the highest you can get in New Jersey: High Point, elevation 1,803 feet. This rural county is also the Jersey dairy champion. Sussex and Warren, south of it on the Delaware side, are well endowed with open spaces, their rolling fields walled in by the Kittatinny Range, and on the west by the Delaware River. The river in this pastoral northern stretch looks young and lovely, almost a wilderness river. In Warren County, where the Delaware makes a westward bend, the Kittatinny Range comes to a sudden, dramatic stop at the Delaware Water Gap. Across the river on the Pennsylvania side, the Poconos do the same. The Gap is a unique place in the world, a magnificent example of a deep, steep cleft cut by a river for about 35 miles between two big mountain ridges. You can stand at a viewpoint and look at the shoulder of a whole mountain, layers of rock tilted skyward as if a giant hand had squeezed it into a sharp fold. The sight is stupendous. The best way to see all this is from the Appalachian Trail, which winds along the Gap on its journey through the East Coast mountains.

If you follow the riverside country up into Sussex County, meandering along the curving, rolling roads that criss-cross the meadows and mountains, you may forget what year it is, even if you are in a horseless carriage. The quiet little villages you go through look more like the early than the late 20th century. The houses, some plain, some with Victorian elaborations, sit sedately by the road with their wrap-around porches like shields against the intrusions of today. The fields and pastures between the towns, and the herds of dairy cattle, add to the sense of peace and permanence.

But Sussex is not just yesterday. Its mountains and lakes and its Appalachian Trail are attractions for the outdoors people of today, those who may work in cities and seek sanctuary once in a while in nature's open places. Natural preserves, parks, and resorts crop up all over Sussex, and its eastern mountains are easily accessible to the great cities of the north coast. Massive new summer and winter recreational developments, like Vernon Valley/Great Gorge, are giving New Jersey's northern interior some of the limelight that has for so long been focused on the glamorous Jersey shore.

The Surf and the Southland

Middle and south Jersey give away nothing to the other areas in variety of natural features, colorful towns, and opportunities for recreation. First, by all odds, is that most famous New Jersey feature, the longest line of sandy beach in the world. Those wide, gently sloping shores reach 127 miles from Sandy Hook, guarding Raritan Bay to Cape May at the southern tip of the state. On the middle and south shore are the barrier beaches, lined with towns that have made beach tans and ocean bathing a hallowed tradition for residents of Atlantic Seaboard cities. Each beach resort seems to have its special clientele, and visitors come from as far away as New England and from points south of New Jersey. The barrier islands form an almost solid line on the more southerly part of this oceanfront. Back of them are the big bays and river estuaries that have been prime sports fishing waters ever since people have known about them.

Island Beach is one of these very long oceanic sand spits, measuring about 20 miles from Point Pleasant to Barnegat Inlet. The inlet to Barnegat Bay is at the southern end, guarded by Barnegat Light, "Old Barney." The lighthouse is the second oldest in the nation, built in 1857-58 after an earlier one at that spot fell into the sea. It was desperately needed long before it was installed, because the shoals just off the Barnegat coast had taken an enormous toll of lives and ships earlier in the century. Today the bayside is a busy harbor during the fine weather, when the marinas of Toms River send forth their fleets of charter and private fishing boats into the waters of Barnegat Bay.

Island Beach State Park occupies the southern half of the barrier island, and has been left largely undeveloped. So it is really quite extraordinary in the context of Jersey's resort-crowded shore. Although there are bathing beaches on it and a road part of the way down its center, the southern end is given over to wildlife and walkers. There are natural areas along most of the bayside, too, and a nature center where the shoreline ecology is explained and given substance in a nature walk.

The beach towns, except for the bigger and more crowded ones, don't seem to change much. As always, they have their boardwalks fronting wide, white-sand beaches, and their genteel-looking, comfortable hotels and cottages to house the vacationers. Night life, and all that, is left to a few of the more elaborate places like Long Branch and Asbury Park up north, and Atlantic City, long-time champion "fun place" of the south shore.

Back on the coastal mainland, the towns are quieter and more like "country." The coastal road (U.S. 9) connects a string of small communities, among them Waretown, Barnegat, Manahawkin, and Staffordville. Though Route 9 is the main street of all of them, it seems to be a different street each time it enters a new town, such is their individual charm. Ten miles north of Atlantic City, the road heads inland around Great Bay, the biggest break in the line of barrier islands, and in a practically untouched part of the coast. Great Bay is a maze of sand bars, slough, channels, salt flats, and marshes, which produces some of the best saltwater sport fishing on the Jersey coast.

If Atlantic City is banking on a new kind of action these days, the quiet little town at the southern end of the shore is doing very well sticking with the old ways. Cape May capitalizes on its ties with the past. The county's namesake town and others, like Ocean City and the Wildwoods, still do things much the way they have for many decades. Their wide beaches have the whitest sand on the whole coast and stretch unbroken for great distances, so on a hot summer weekend the visitors outnumber the residents many times over. But at dusk, when the sunbathers are applying the liniment to scorched skin and silently stealing away, quiet returns.

Cape May is famous all over the country for its historic Victorian elegance. The town's old-fashioned look once was close to putting it out of business until people, residents and visitors alike, began to realize that old wasn't so bad after all and rediscovered Cape May's quiet charm. Now the town is self-consciously preserving its marvelous old wood hotels and residences, some of pre-Civil War vintage. Along the gas-lighted streets, the intricate elaborations of these gorgeous old structures show up to great advantage. Imaginative carpentry, of the sort that went into some of these places, may never be seen again. Cape May is a living museum and a great beach town all at the same time. Famous folks and plain folks have been coming here since 1766, sometimes from far away. These days the Cape sometimes speaks with a French-Canadian accent, and some of its restaurants cater to the tastes of the visitors from the north who seem to like its style. There may be a little of New Orleans in it, or at least some of the Old South. It is, after all, below the Mason-Dixon line.

Philadelphians, from their advance post across the Delaware River, have long regarded the south Jersey shore almost as their private preserve. But many pay scant attention to the countryside they go through to get to the cool, green Atlantic. This part of New Jersey is more than worthy to be noticed for its fertile fields and vast wilderness pines.

The garden spot of the Garden State is the group of southwestern counties that grow all those farm products: Gloucester, Cumberland, Salem, and Burlington. The last named is the largest of Jersey's 21 counties. That is *one* of its distinctions. Another is in what takes up more than two-thirds of Burlington. The Pine barrens, or The Pines, as they are usually called, are an immense swatch of largely undifferentiated pine forest that is not officially wilderness, but is so pristine and thinly inhabited that it qualifies as such. In the most densely populated state in the nation, the forest contains an average of only 15 people in a square mile. The Pines cover more than 600,000 acres, a size category similar to Yosemite and other big national parks. About a thousand square miles of the Pine Barrens are still wild, although "The Pines" cover a lot more area than that. In some places little towns have grown up around the lakes hidden in the wood. Amazingly, huge chunks of the Barrens — thousands of acres — have no human inhabitants at all.

A major portion of The Pines is now protected in the Wharton State Forest. Some protection would seem to be needed, because development keeps chewing away at the edges. These pinelands are valuable as much for what is under them as for their visible part. The sandy soil absorbs rainwater like a blotter, and underneath it is one of the world's biggest aquifers — a tremendous natural lake of the purest water. The Pines have their own river system, too. No water comes into the Barrens from outside areas that could carry pollution. The streams of the forest are therefore perfectly pure, although they are often characterized by a dark color leeched from nearby oaks and cedars, and from the iron-rich earth. But pollution could easily arrive, because the porous sand that lets in the rainwater allows entry also to the pollutants.

The water table is always near the surface, as many boggy areas attest. In the past century, cultivation of the forest's wild cranberry bogs was begun, and since then the pine bogs have been a major producer of cranberries.

The Pine Barrens are still a place of mystery, almost roadless except around the edges. Pathways through the heart of the area are mere sandy tracks that were established long, long ago. Hikers and hunters still get lost in The Pines. Such wilderness is beyond price these days. That it should exist right here in a state where all the action is, is one of the continuing astonishments that New Jersey keeps pulling out of her bag of tricks.